Pressed Flowers:
Poems of Resistance

John Eppel

Edited by Tendai Rinos Mwanaka

Mwanaka Media and Publishing Pvt Ltd,
Chitungwiza Zimbabwe
*
Creativity, Wisdom and Beauty

Publisher:
Mwanaka Media and Publishing Pvt Ltd *(Mmap)*
24 Svosve Road, Zengeza 1
Chitungwiza Zimbabwe

mwanaka@yahoo.com
mwanaka13@gmail.com
www.africanbookscollective.com/publishers/mwanaka-media-and-publishing
https://facebook.com/MwanakaMediaAndPublishing/

Distributed in and outside N. America by African Books Collective
orders@africanbookscollective.com
www.africanbookscollective.com

ISBN: 978-1-77929-615-3
EAN: 9781779296153

© John Eppel 2020

All rights reserved.
No part of this book may be reproduced or transmitted in any form or by any means, mechanical or electronic, including photocopying and recording, or be stored in any information storage or retrieval system, without written permission from the publisher

DISCLAIMER
All views expressed in this publication are those of the author and do not necessarily reflect the views of *Mmap*.

Versions of these poems have appeared online and in hard copy in numerous magazines and anthologies

Mwanaka Media and Publishing Editorial Board:

Publisher/ Editor-in-Chief: Tendai Rinos Mwanaka
mwanaka13@gmail.com
East Africa and Swahili Literature: Dr Wanjohi wa Makokha
makokha.justus@ku.ac.ke
East Africa English Literature: Andrew Nyongesa (PhD student)
nyongesa55.andrew@gmail.com
East Africa and Children Literature: Richard Mbuthia
ritchmbuthia@gmail.com
Legal Studies and Zimbabwean Literature: Jabulani Mzinyathi
jabumzi@gmail.com
Economics, Development, Environment and Zimbabwean Literature: Dr Ushehwedu Kufakurinani ushehwedu@gmail.com
History, Politics, International relations and South African Literature: Antonio Garcia antoniogarcia81@yahoo.com
North African and Arabic Literature: Fethi Sassi
sassifathi62@yahoo.fr
Gender and South African Literature: Abigail George
abigailgeorge79@gmail.com
Francophone and South West African Literature: Nsah Mala
nsahmala@gmail.com
West Africa Literature: Macpherson Okpara
chiefmacphersoncritic@gmail.com
Media studies and South African Literature: Mikateko Mbambo
me.mbambo@gmail.com
Portuguese and West Africa Literature: Daniel da Purificação
danieljose26@yahoo.com.br

Table of Contents

Introduction..viii
Spoils of War...1
Star of Bethlehem..4
Thin White Line..6
Jacaranda..7
Appropriating the Land...8
Our Last Hot Spell...9
Rhodesian Lullaby...10
The Midnight Blooming...11
Pioneer Woman with Four Jacks...................................12
Call it 'In Memory of Josiah Tongogara'.........................14
Tracks I Remember...15
My Father's tool Box..16
Flower Poem...17
Retreat...19
Shards..22
Cewale..23
Pungwe..24
Winter in Matabeleland..25
Songbirds...27
Bhalagwe Blues..28
The Bones Will Speak..30
Waiting for the Bus...31
You Ask We Why..34
Coming Home to Tea..35
Sonnet with One Unstated Line...................................36
Practising Scales...37
Song for WOZA...40

Border Jumping..........41
Via Dolorosa..........42
Vendor and Child..........44
Bring Back Our Girls..........46
Culture..........48
Broke Buttock Blues..........49
Ghostly Galleon..........51
Waiting..........53
Sick at Heart..........54
An Awkward Gait..........56
Afrika..........57
Malnourished Sonnet..........58
Dog..........59
Crunch Time..........60
The Clothes Dictators Wear..........61
Manifesto..........62
The Dog Meat Vendor..........64
For the Disappeared..........65
Obnubilation..........66
Soft as Wool..........67
Disconnected Policeman..........68
Mother Nature's Warning..........69
My Uncle the Minister..........70
No Time to Bleed..........71
The Ballad of Prophet Squeegee..........72
Who is Protecting Them?..........73
Wind behaving badly..........74
English Sonnet in Broken Metre..........75
The Honourable Minister Speaks..........76
Five Five-line Stanzas..........79
Those About to Play..........80
Brats..........81
Yet Another Flower Poem..........82

The Coming of the Rains..84

Epilogue..*85*
Seeking Identity...85
Mmap New African Poets Series...86

Introduction

There is method in Ophelia's madness when she hands each member of her close associates a particular flower. Her brother, Laertes gets rosemary, which conveys a message of remembrance. He also gets a pansy, symbol of sorrow. She is addressing him more as a lover than a brother. This is foreshadowed early on in the play when she offers her brother the 'key' to her 'chaste treasure'. She gives Claudius, the King, fennel and columbines. The former suggests flattery, the latter, unfaithfulness. Gertrude, the Queen (Hamlet's mother), gets rue. Ophelia keeps some for herself. Rue is associated with sorrow and repentance. 'You must wear your rue with a difference' says Ophelia to the Queen, but she doesn't specify which difference. That message she conveys in her next offering: a daisy. This flower stands for deception. The one flower she does not have to distribute, symbol of fidelity, is the violet.

I choose this example from one of the foremost texts of the western literary canon deliberately. When I started school in the 50s my teachers were all British expatriates who instilled in me, through songs, pictures and, above all, poetry, a yearning for aspects of nature that did not occur in hot, drought-prone Matabeleland: snow, nightingales, daffodils.... As I grew older and more politically aware, I chose not to discard these colonial images embedded in conventional forms like sonnets and ballads, but to parody them as a means of self-mockery. But that would have been too easy. Yes, they are parodies, but they are also, and profoundly, a means of self-respect, a pride in my craft.

I'm not the first person to imagine my poems as flowers. Think of Baudelaire's 'Les Fleur du Mal'. In his dedication he describes them as 'sickly flowers'. For him they signified decadence and they ushered in, according to T. S. Eliot, Modernism. For me flowers have a number of significations: transience, female sexuality, 'wise passiveness', domestic life, creativity; but in this selection their chief significance is resistance – to tyranny, greed, hypocrisy, and self-righteousness. We press flowers because we want to make a special moment last. We press them within the covers of books. If you write a poem about a flower, you have a meta-text: a 'flower' about a flower, both 'pressed' within the pages of a book. Think too of the association of 'press' with 'print'. While every poem in this selection is a 'pressed flower', only a portion of them are meta-texts, and those mainly in the pre-Independence poems. The flowers on the cover belong to the Sabi Star, Adenium obesum – the ostensible subject of my poem, 'Spoils of War'. If I were present at Ophelia's flower parade I would have hoped for a gladiolus, my mother's favourite, symbol of resilience, remembering, and, dare I say it?- infatuation. It means 'sword', which is an anagram of 'words'.

SPOILS OF WAR

It took me all afternoon, in full view
of swaggering Frelimo, to dig up
that girl-sized stem. What a hullabaloo,
I thought, would this create in peacetime. Sup-
pose they invoked the law (Government Notice
14 of 1975)? I
had no permit, and they'd certainly miss
this fatso, though it grows abundantly
in Vila Salazar. *Adenium*
Obesum enjoys the hot, dry lowveld;
it would flourish in Colleen Bawn, become
a talking point at the Club.
                                                So I knelt
beside this hyper-bole and hugged it out
of the earth. With its final give I gave
and we tumbled like lovers, till a shout
from our camp warned that I was in grave
danger, Frelimo were watching. "Get in
you titface." I took my loot, and the spade
for digging bunkers, (oops and my weapon),
and stumbled for cover.
                                That night we made
a sweep of the T.T.L. Our section
was ill-prepared. None of us had wanted
to carry the big-gun. We had to spin
for it. I lost. I wished that thing planted
like a Sabi Star. None of us took bangs.
Too dangerous. Besides we needed the space
in our kidney pouches for gin meringues
and quarterjacks of Limosin – in case

of snake bite!
                    In a clinking of bottles
and a clanking of weaponry we steer
our tackies, discussing Aristotle's
Poetics. Tragedy should excite fear
and pity: "Our pity is awakened
by undeserved misfortune, and our fear
by that of someone just like ourselves." Tinned
thoughts these, at this time. Shall we squeeze a tear
or two. Army life makes rat-packs of our
minds.
            The LMG drags me through the bush,
its muzzle close to the ground. A sour,
smoky stink of terror checks it. I push
forward, then flatten in a commotion
that splits a bag of raisins in my brain.

When the screaming starts, I have a notion,
lying on my back – horizontal rain
of tracer bullets just above my nose –
a notion that some cattle have been shot.
I start feeling pity and fear for those
poor bellowing beasts. Surely that is not
a human sound. The screams go on all night.

Next morning our section finds their shelter,
fifteen metres from where we lay. The sight
of corpses, and their smell, like an abattoir,
forces warm pilchards into my throat. "Look
at that," says Sarge, "a Tokarev pistol
still in its grease." He pockets it. They take
a portable radio, a fistful
of rounds, and empty AK magazine,

five teeth, a penis, a number of ears,
and a picture of someone in a green
uniform. Sarge tells me to save my tears
for the civilians these gooks have slaughtered.
But I am not thinking of them, and I
cannot explain that I am being purged
of my Rhodesianism. That ugly
word with its jagged edge is opening
me. Through a haze of baked beans in chili
sauce I move to the past tense.

                                          The going
was tough but at last I had my frilly-
petalled (highly protected) succulent
shrub buried up to its neck in granite
subsoil. *Adenium* does not transplant
well, but this one flourished. You can see it
there today. It flowers in September.
And if ever you live in our old home —
the one in the village — please remember
not to over-water my cuddlesome
stump. And if you are bothered by the law,
tell them that the plant is a spoil of war.

Editor's Note: Frelimo — Front for the Liberation of Mozambique. Adenium Obesum — Sabi Star. A succulent shrub or small tree bearing pink and white flowers in late winter. T.T.L. — Tribal Trust Lands: the name in the 1960s and 1970s for rural land set apart for black communal occupation. Limosin — A cheap brandy LMG — Light machine gun - Gooks — Rhodesian army slang for guerrillas adopted from the US army in Vietnam.

STAR OF BETHLEHEM

We called it that when we were very young,
before we'd learned about epiphanies
though Father's crackly 78, sung
by Richard Crooks, the school nativities,
the "sorrowing, sighing, bleeding
dying" of our Colleen Bawn carol choir –
beer soaked bass, and baritone receding,
sopranos launched by Aunty Nola's higher
than hyena hallelujah - all these
were pretty damn close to epiphanies.

My mother banned it from the flower beds;
to her it ranked with stinkblaar as a chronic
garden weed: the glossy leaves, the flat heads
in white and purple, smelling of tonic,
she did not hesitate to destroy. She
called them "missionary plants", the housewives'
bane. Yet these flowers of nativity
which, healers claim, are saving many lives:
curing cancer and Hodgkin's disease,
are pretty damn close to epiphanies.

It took one long day to dig that bunker.
I broke the handle of my spade. The ground
was rock hard. Nothing grew there but paper
thorns and, wonderfully: five petals, round
and white and smelling of tonic, opened flat
against the sky: a Star of Bethlehem.
I picked it and stuffed it in my combat

jacket on top of a phosphorus bomb.
I want to tell you: moments such as these
are pretty damn close to epiphanies.

THIN WHITE LINE

You, Great-Grandfather:
colonial volunteer;
Ladysmith, Waggon Hill, Spion Kop;
(killed in action):
you came home a hero.

You, Oupa:
despatch rider;
Windhoek, Swakopmund, Tsumeb;
(wounded in the hand):
you came home a hero.

You, Dad:
lorry driver;
Tobruk, Alamein, Halfaya Pass;
(slightly shell-shocked)
you came home a hero.

You, son:
rifleman;
Plumtree, Bubi, Vila Salazar;
(confused):
you came home a polecat.

JACARANDA

Not for that Matabele the plopping
sub-resonance of Brazilian blue
blooms, as clapperless as the bell his mum
once used to call her boy: 'Hosea, bring
checha lo second course'; which now stands sprue-
marked, missed, achromatistous, and dumb
like Ndimande, who kept a large pair
of scissors in his eyes. Not for this 'ou'
your late September flush of beautiful
violet-blue blossoms, a colour so rare,
so indescribably rare, and so, oh
so apt to rhyme with veranda. Your bull-
necked, drum-thighed Rhodesian in a powder
blue safari-suit two sizes too small;
bignonia shaped, tight forward, mauled, rucked
representative; no one is louder
when it comes to curling the lips at all
things bright and beautiful than your product
of Plumtree, of Falcon, of Milton; your
small-but-vigorous cocked, vast bummed hero.
Not for Hosea - they'll reap the whirlwind -
Ndimande either, your 'sweep flower
off lo driveway checha'. Why must they grow
things you can't eat or smoke or sell? What kind
of boss - stab, stab - is this who worships trees,
with flowers that make work and sting like bees.

APPROPRIATING THE LAND

We did dams, brown roads with middle-
mannetjies and suppressed
ant hills. We introduced fiddle-
wood for its autumn-stressed
hues and the way its falling petals
sounded like rain. We did
chip geysers, Blair toilets, landfills….
We mapped grid after grid.

We erected bossy warnings
with words like 'forbidden'
and 'only'. We blue-pencilled springs,
used an ancient midden
to support a retaining wall,
re-named *utshani*. We did
Napier Avenue, Town hall…
planning grid after grid.

We wrote poems about sunsets,
jacarandas, blue skies,
the dispositions of our pets,
and the fish eagle's cries.
We wrote about bitter longing,
sometimes florid, sometimes terse –
metaphors and symbols thronging,
verse after verse after verse.

OUR LAST HOT SPELL

This is our last hot spell for, let me see,
a moment, two seasons, and eternity.
The haze, as thick as cotton waste, plugs
our senses. A wind stirs, a strychnos shrugs
off dying leaves; slow fruit sickens
and drops to inspire men and concuss chickens.

The late sun smears with gore our senses;
a wind stirs dislodging rust from fences
that keep out bushveld. Memories turn
like falling leaves, to smoulder and burn.
This is our last hot spell for, let me see,
a moment, two seasons, and eternity.

RHODESIAN LULLABY

Like shrapnel from an old bomb, we scatter
to other lands, delivering reasons.
On our elbows and our knees, a season's
grass-burns. On the backs of our hands, faces,
and necks – the first traces of skin cancer.
Yes, we're Rhodesians. Does it matter?

Even our children have learned not to cry
for their puppies' graves. The women weep
no more for their gardens. And the men sleep
less fitfully on their way to Smithland
or Salisbury-by-the-sea. A boozy band
of rebels, we fought the world and lost. Why

should it matter? Rhodesians never die.
From our mouths flat patriotisms slide
tight as trouser-legs, unbending as pride.
Stories of war spread like phosphorus
to our eyes. In a trickling of pus
and blood down cheeks, we shout our lullaby.

Our wallets were fat, our bellies fatter.
Memories of war slip like envelopes
under the doors of our minds. Each one copes
in his own way – a defiant slogan
on a T-shirt, the old flag printed on
a dishcloth ... hush now ... it doesn't matter.

THE MIDNIGHT BLOOMING

Although that night, beyond the pitch
of ululating strings, was dim
enough to veil the twinkle
of a riot squad; although
the atmospheric pressure
on the square inch of my brain
was more than fourteen comma
seven pounds, my stanzas,
O my stanzas, were as light
as plastic bucket blue.

Although the band that played before
had twanged 'Amandla' to a drift
of flowers sweetly clenched; and then
'Awethu' wafted thousand
thousand perfumes in reply;
although the rain came down in dog-
bites, and the midnight blossoms dripped
a crimson song, my stanzas,
O my stanzas, were as pale
as plastic bucket blue.

PIONEER WOMAN WITH FOUR JACKS

And then she'd cite her hero, Cecil Rhodes:
'You spoke of them,' she would apostrophize,
as Africa's greatest asset; but as far
as houseboys are concerned, my boy, you are
Africa's smelliest ass. And then my grin
would fade as she recalled the wagon trek
from Beaufort West to Kuruman, and then

to Bulawayo via Khama's land,
as Kipling puts it somewhere. Kipling is
her favourite poet, his 'If' she knows by heart.
Recalled the birth of her child, stillborn, in the shade
of a wait-a-bit tree – she would have named him John.
Recalled the death of her husband, John: 'He was killed
by a lion.' And then she'd quote, 'So little done,

so much to do' , and ring the bell for the houseboy,
John, and order tea, and lemonade
For piccanin baas John, and scones with home-made
marula jelly. I'd grin at him, he'd grin
at me, she'd disapprove, give a terrible sigh,
resume her game of Patience, placing Jack
on Jack on Jack, and turning up a Jack.

I and the Black Poet

I have my subject in focus,
now I must focus my poem.
It's a memory of crocus
bulbs. The memory is dim

but on page ninety-seven
of What Flower is That?
there's a picture of a pink one.
The petals are opened – not flat
like a daisy, or just,
like a protea, but halfway
like me. Now, with care, I must
arrange my words so that the 'gay
little flowers…pop right out
of the ground in earliest spring.'
Shall they be white, or violet
or yellow or blue? And shining?
Shall they shining? Not bright
like stars, or dullish like paper,
but halfway like spoons. O the light
in the pink of this picture
is lovely. It half opens
me to the sky. Like silver-striped
leaves my arms follow seasons
never cold enough for a typed
memory of crocuses.
Too hot, this earth, for words to grow
Into my bulbs. He focuses
on Sharpeville and Soweto.

CALL IT 'IN MEMORY OF GENERAL JOSIAH TONGOGARA'

With your permission, William Butler Yeats?
And yours, Mr Davie? Is it Donald Alfred?
I have set up these three sophisticates:
types of thin-lipped greed, authenticated
not by art but by their thin-lipped times.

First the cash-box bandit, Cecil John,
tossed like coins a thousand thousand crimes
that fell on heads and tails, or rolled along
those hunters' tracks pressing northward from the Cape,
acquiring land for a promise and a song.

Next, guilty of riot-een, loot-een, rape-
een in nearly every speech, the Wrong
but Honourable Ian Douglas Smith,
extant. Fearless as a tiger, he did
a lot of bona fide damage with

the likes of me, in this set up, the third
and final pair of lips, so tight they'd break
the circle of a rhyme, so thin they'd cut
a kiss in two, so sorry they'd embarrass
General Josiah Tongogara, extinct.

TRACKS I REMEMBER

Paths with banks of tick-heavy grass tilting
to caress the thigh; roads where dipping
hornbills lead the way, mopani scrub on
either side; tok-tokkies doing headstands,
their fused wings harder than fingernails, tap-
tapping messages of love; antlion
larvae (doodlebugs) crafting pits of death
where the critical angle of repose
slides crawling insects to their doom;
stink of formic acid, of resin, of
crushed locusts, wings in threatening display.

Paths with trip-wires working an explosion;
banks of whispering gun-muzzles, safety
catches clicking like beetles; roads going
nowhere, primed; the relative safety of
middle mannetjies where devil thorns cling
to combat boots; farm gates, not quite open,
not quite shut, availing detonators;
cadres, exposed like anthills, keeping still,
stiller than puff adders basking, spiders
playing dead; stink of fear, of corpses
with hand grenades in threatening display.

My Father's Tool Box

This is the story that the Sandman tells:
It started as an ammunition box,
a wooden crate packed with howitzer shells -
part of a plan to rout the Desert Fox.

Your father found it empty, discarded,
hard by the railhead at Mersa Matruh.
Intact, though with a slightly damaged lid,
it kept his puttees from the foggy dew.

After the war he brought the plunder home,
repaired the lid, renewed the rope handles,
painted it red and packed it with cheap, chrome-
plated tools, grease, spare matches and candles.

When fate came calling, he left it to you,
you emptied it (that smell of oil, that hint
of cordite), scraped it and painted it blue,
filled it with cuddly toys and peppermint,

filled it with dressing-up clothes, porcelain
dolls, the little red hen, the gingerbread
man; filled it with soldiers made out of tin...
Sandman is back in the realm of the dead.

Flower Poem

How, I ask, can such perfection grow?
Sure, I can see how the word grew,
though the initial 'D' is obscure;
genus Asphodelus; now genus

Narcissus (also called Lent Lily).
But that bloom looks like a plastic
candle-holder for a giant ('s)
birthday cake. It's too damn yellow

for one thing, and for another
it's already been done by Herrick
and Wordsworth. The only poetic
thing left about a daffodil

is that it almost rhymes with … I can't say it.
'You can buy them,' said the woman
from - don't you forget it - Rhodesia,
whose bunch of five I'd admired

in the lift - 'you can buy them from
the old kaffir-girl in the street.'
I smiled bravely. 'Yes, aren't they lovely.
Ten cents each. Don't let her cheat you.'

I bought one with a broken stem
for half the price. Her eyes were yellow
with smoke. She was bent like the handle
of a candle-holder. 'Master?'

She called me master. Bravely I smiled.
It was the last flower of her day
She could go home. A blanketful
of wrinkles and an empty tin

moving slowly down Prince Street. This poem
is about the space between me
and my subject. This poem is the space
between me and my subject. I can't say it.

Retreat
It's whimsical of me to feel afraid
of an English night on a Shropshire farm;
the wildest beasts are a Labrador, spayed,
and a dairyman with a shrivelled arm.
The Friesland cows are safely in their shed,
the lapwing's day-long din is stilled; no owl's
eerie screech unnerves; not a mouse is dead –
then why this levitation of my bowels?

No AK47s in this night,
no Shona spirit mediums to haunt
my settler soul, no airplanes set alight
by the screams of butchered friends, and no taunt
of 'Zimbabwe'. There are no elephants
to nudge down the oaks or to tap a tusk
into my groin; no cobras lying aslant
my stride, scales glinting in a loop of dusk.

Then why do I feel this night too tightly
buttoned at my throat, this vault of a room,
Its elbow-pressing walls, too close to me?
The television will relieve my gloom.
I dive for its button and with almost
love, await the comfort of its flicker.
Songs of Praise from Romsey Abbey. The ghost
of a memory undertakes to stir ….

It's a term-time Sunday at Milton School;
the heat of the day has let go my nose
but lingers on in the quadrangle's pool
of tar, and the parched voices of pied crows
patrolling Selborne Avenue for spread-

eagled frogs. Today I'm on flag duty;
it must be lowered at six o' clock dead.
The bugle boy will keep me company.

As the shadows lengthen across the quad
I take my place at the Union Jack,
steady the rope, watch for the bugler's nod ...
he wets his lips, I give a little slack,
he checks his watch, he nods ... he pitches flats
and sharps clear over the roofs of the town.
The flag comes creaking slow ... tat tara, tat
tara, tat tara, tat-tat tara ... down,

down, down it crumples, into the cuddle
of my arms. I fold it as the last keen
statement (lest ye forget) of the bugle
suspends itself like a hammock between
past and present .... The school hymn is finished,
the organ agitates a tremolo.
My times are, my spaces, are diminished.
I am afraid. I have nowhere to go.
The Lizards at the View of the World

The bald porcupine, Inungu, has grown a
a bristle. It looks like a cross from here.
Inantaba, set farther on, cries birds
to me on a purple-crested morning.

I take two steps back and trip over Rhodes'
grave. The lichen comes alive in a rush
of lizards: orange, blue, yellowstone grey:
Platysaurus Capensis, I presume?

I wonder what titbits you accepted
from Uncle Cecil and Leander Starr?
Still do, perhaps? This dwala is casting
its cutis perpetually. Who knows

what networks have spread in the scurf where they
lie? I tap the lid with my mind's finger;
it rings like a cash register. I turn
back to the hills, my eyes westering deep.

The Maleme valley. Rowland and Liz.
Willie's framed photograph taken from Black
Eagle Lodge; Mrs Hep's cold beetroot soup;
the smell of spilt beer, and smoke from braai grids -

they pack like pain the cavities of my
past. My tongue explores my teeth and I dis-
lodge a piece of gristle. I take it out
and flick it on the rock. The lizards freeze

for an instant into lichen - then pounce.
The have grown quite used to brooding spirits,
and I shall always love them for staying
on; and it is for them that I'll return.

SHARDS

In a low country clear of the hills,
near where the Shashani River spills
in a good season - discovered there,
Early Stone Age tools, hand-axes, rare
now that plunderers, from the Trekker
(known to his foes as *Ndaleka*),
through the likes of Carl Mauch, Thomas Baines,
to Cecil John Rhodes and other stains
of imperial ink, have come and gone,
some under the ground and some upon.

Rare too are the human bits that in
more recent times, still adorned with skin,
in that low country of thorns and spines,
just clear of the hills, long worked-out mines
like Antelope, there discovered,
dropped down abandoned shafts and covered
with leafy branches, clumps of grass, stones -
because the police have moved the bones,
some muscle still attached to a groin,
and a 1980 five cent coin.

CEWALE

A river runs past girls and boys, and swerves
as if to miss the donkey cart trotting
out of Lupane. That hint of rotting
faces, breasts, backsides...mouldering bones, serves
to remind us of *Gukurahundi*:
early rain that washes away the dust
of harvests, the chaff of narrowing lust.
A figure out of *Spiritus Mundi*,
which more than troubles the collective sight,
a figure of unlimited power,
his balls grenades, his cock a bayonet,
always confident, always in the right,
chuckles as he plucks a bank-side flower
and tucks it coyly in his epaulette.

PUNGWE
   [Matobo, 1984]

Masoja were speaking in Shona, their sticks
were *mopane* - that wood is like iron;
broke all my arms and this leg that can't bend;
yes, fan belts, *umfo*, and kicking with boots;
made us undress and do sex with a goat;
then with our bums; sang: *"Pasi LoNkomo."*
But first they *khetha* some youngsters, not me,
was my brother, my cousin, my neighbours...
on one side putting three, other side three;
then they give me a pick and a *fotshol*,
say dig, and I dig; on this side one grave,
other side one, not deep, to end of my
 thing; yes, naked in front of our mothers,
our sisters; *gebha* as deep as the end
of your thing: *mbolo*. Made them to kneel
by the side of the graves; shooting them dead.
We were dancing and singing, and screaming
with pain; they beat us and kicked us for hours,
umfo; yes, calling us dissidents,
whilest we sang: *"Pambili LoMugabe."*

Winter in Matabeleland, 1987

The airlock in our hose pipe won't be heard
for another season;
the spider in our spout, he won't be stirred
for another season.

The Zanu/Zapu dialogue is dead
until what rains?
The Somabula Flats are tinctured red
until what rains?

On caps of wind the migrant swallows soar:
will they return?
Our soldiers guard the Beira Corridor:
will they return?

I found a rusty bayonet in the yard:
lest we forget;
some two-by-four and half a playing card:
lest we forget.

We watch our garden dying flower by flower...
perhaps the spring?
The water table falling hour by hour...
perhaps the spring?

There's part of a heart on the card I found:
does it portend?

The Rhodies rev their Hondas, southward bound:
does it portend?

Our new born baby squints her eyes to see
(love, light the fire)
her two-dimensional security.
Love, light the fire.

SONGBIRDS

She was harbouring a dissident in her womb;
they unseamed her with a bayonet;
it dangled from her umbilicus
like a jolly-jumper.
And the doves sang:
gukura
hundi,
gukura
hundi.

Little children of "traitors",
transformed by heavy blows -
they use branches, batons, iron bars -
to pumpkins about to spill their seeds.
And the hornbills cry:
*Vana**
we nyoka
inyoka
wo futi

*The children of snakes are also snakes

BHALAGWE* BLUES

They kidnap these tourists, blame Zipra, blame me,
they kidnap these tourists, blame Zipra, blame me,
I say I am innocent, let me go free.

They laugh, call me dissident, spit in my face,
they laugh, call me dissident, spit in my face,
they force me to go to a terrible place.

We dig many graves every day in the sun,
we dig many graves every day in the sun,
they tease us then kill us, they do it for fun.

We cook for them sadza, we polish their boots,
we cook for them sadza, we polish their boots,
red beret, he laughs, then he shouts, then he shoots.

They tie rubber strips 'round my balls, and then beat,
they tie rubber strips 'round my balls, and then beat,
when they burst cannot pray, cannot sleep, cannot eat.

Putting wires to my ears, to my mouth, to my back,
putting wires to my ears, to my mouth, to my back,
my body it jump like *umvundla***, then crack.

Pushed a cloth in my mouth, poured water, I choke,
pushed a cloth in my mouth, poured water, I choke,
jumping my tummy till everything broke.

They left me to die in the shade of a tree,
they left me to die in the shade of a tree,
they said, you can go, picannin, you are free.

*Notorious torture camp used by the Fifth Brigade during Gukurahundi
**hare

THE BONES WILL SPEAK

The eyes will close, the lips will fold,
The ears will cauliflower,
But the bones, the bones, the bones will speak
For ever and an hour.

The nose will block, the tongue will curl,
The taste of figs turn sour,
But the bones, the bones, the bones will speak
For ever and an hour.

The crotch will rust, the nipples flake,
The whole demeanour cower,
But the bones, the bones, the bones will speak
For ever and an hour.

WAITING FOR THE BUS

All along the road from Bulawayo
to Gwanda or Matopos or Vic Falls;
at bus-stops, lay-bys, under shadeless trees,
the people wait beside their bundled things.
All day long they wait, and sometimes all night
too, and the next day – anxiously waiting.

Waiting for the public transport to stop
and let them in and take them home. Waiting
with babies to nurse, children to comfort
and feed, chickens, the occasional goat.
They have learned to come prepared, with blankets,
izinduku, pots for cooking sadza.

Waiting for ZUPCO or SHU-SHINE, AJAY,
to get them to their Uncle's funeral,
their cousin's wedding, their baby brother's
baptism. Waiting with the new Camper Vans
cruising by. Anxious to be at work on
time. Anxious not to lose their jobs. Waiting.

They take their time now not by wrist-watches
but by the sun and the stars and the moon;
by the appearance of the mopani worms;
by the ripening of marula fruit;
by the coming of the rains. Not by bus
timetables but by birth, marriage and death.

And while they wait they count the jets that fly

to Harare and Johannesburg.
Liverish businessmen sucking whiskies
are in these jets. And Chefs with mistresses
wearing the latest digital watches,
Digital dolly-birds. All carry brief-

cases with combination locks, and next
to nothing inside: dark glasses perhaps;
and a newspaper to study the Stock
Exchange; something digital, perhaps, for
calculating profit . . . and more profit.
It's something for people to do while

they wait – counting the jets high overhead.
Often the vapour trails are the only
clouds in the sky. No Forex for buses,
They tell us, but the five-star hotels go
up, and another Boeing is purchased.
All day they wait; all night; long suffering.

And when, at last, a bus does stop, its tyres
are likely to be bald, its brakes likely
to be held together with wire, its body
battered, belching clouds of brain-tightening,
lung-collapsing smoke. Who's responsible?
"Not me," says the Chef dipping his fingers

in his girl-friend's cocktail, shifting his vast
belly, vast enough to accommodate
at least seven baby goats. "Don't look at
me," says the Managing Director, "my
bottom line is profit. I owe it to

the shareholders. Another whisky please."

And I don't think it is going to be any
different tomorrow or the next day
or the next. The time of sweet-becoming
is over. For those millions who depend
on buses, nothing has changed; only their
expectations have once again been dashed.

The time of bitter arrival is here:
not safe new buses, but the amassing
of personal wealth, the cultivation
of another crop of heroes. Street
names change, statues change; hotels go up, jets
go up, and the people go on waiting.

YOU ASK ME WHY

Tall trees with elbows stretch against the sky
to tickle breezes as they giggle by,
and catch the sunlight's gaudy yellow glare
with leaves as bright as polished silverware.
The grass is long and thick and golden green
with crowds of peeping cosmos in-between
the wiry tufts and blades. But on the ground
are plastic bags and beer cans littered round
like ID photos at the Lost and Found.
And that is why I push my glasses off and turn away
before I lose that light, that glimmer, of a lovely day.

Coming Home to Tea

A Heuglin's robin flying low salutes
us as we cycle up the driveway, home.
The dogs pretend to sleep, but cock their ears
and thump their tails. One cat is on the roof,
another stalks the shadow of a cloud.
The rooster flaps his wings as if to say,
'You're welcome, but remember who's in charge!'
And smell that blossom! Is it marigold?

The crested barbet's clock alarm goes off
and wakes a bloukop basking in the sun.
A drongo taunts a hoopoe, steals its worm,
dive-bombs the sprinkler, terrifies the cat
on the warm tin roof. From the kitchen comes
the smell of biscuits baking. Cinnamon
is in the air, and ginger, nutmeg, cloves;
and listen to that kettle singing: 'Tea!'

Beyond the picket, mothers thin as sticks,
unreflecting eyes, aphonic babies,
all but empty plastic bags; and fathers
ashen, no longer grim, no longer keen
for work or football; only the half-jack
half-concealed; and children kicking at stones,
chewing grass, briefly looking up as they
catch the scent of spicy biscuits and tea.

SONNET WITH ONE UNSTATED LINE

See the shambling gait of the unemployed,
the vacant stare of the dispossessed;
the plastic bags by breezes buoyed
or, when evening settles, at rest.
Hear the cry of hornbills lost in yards
of rubble and rags, to split the ears
of those who stand and watch; and the guards
unguarded, hammering, hammering.
Smell the blood and mucous, ashes damp;
breath of birds turned children clamouring,
children clamouring. A tyrant's stamp:
a boot, a fist, a fourteen pounder:
come and witness our city flounder.

Practising Scales

I

On the rugby fields of Spreckley

Rhodesian manhood pounds;

On the Colenbrander Oval

Rhodesian spunk abounds.

At Victoria Olympic Pool

The free-style swimmers poise;

St Mary's English roses

Are mulched by 'garden boys'.

There are redheads on the lawn court

And blondies on the clay,

And bouncers in the cricket nets,

And golfers 'making hay'.

II

On the rugby fields of Spreckley

A crop of mealies grows;

On the Colenbrander Oval

The peanut blossom blows.

The Victoria Olympic Pool
Is stocked with silver bream;
St Mary's English roses
with izintethe teem.
There are layers on the lawn court
And broilers on the clay;
The cricket nets grow cabbages,
The golf course harvests hay.

III
On the rugby fields of Spreckley
The mealie stalks are dead;
On the Colenbrander Oval
The hungry beg for bread.

The Victoria Olympic Pool
Is a giant garbage mound,
St Mary's English roses
A patch of barren ground.

There are termites on the clay court
And termites on the lawn;
The cricket nets grow prickly pears,
The golf course harvests thorn.

SONG FOR WOZA*

Women of this land arise,
fling your windows open wide,
let the breeze of change, denied,
let it take you by surprise.
Amandla omama!

Let it take you to the streets,
walk for freedom, walk for peace,
disarm with charm the armed police,
give them flowers and home-made treats.
Amandla abafazi!

Let it blow through corridors
where men of power strap their boots,
sip hot liquor, smoke cheroots,
boast of virgins and of whores.
Amandla amankazana!

Let it, when you go to jail,
keep your foreheads cool, your hearts,
keep refreshed the gentler arts –
then let it grow into a gale.
Amandla yesifazane!

*Women Of Zimbabwe Arise - courageous activists, forever being imprisoned

BORDER JUMPING

Once all set about with fever trees
where hippos squeaked like rubber toys
and crocs gave rides to girls and boys:
the Limpopo River, if you please.

Now the banks are greasy with leftovers:
a doek, a hair extension, a knitted
bootie (pink for girls), a broken sandal.

In the high and far-off times, the croc
he lengthened the elephant's nose,
vamped it from a boot to a hose,
stretched it to a stocking from a sock.

Now a decayed, half-eaten corpse, grey-green,
lies unidentified near the bottly
tree with eight leaves only, and twisty roots.

Once long ago in colonial times
they lied to us in clever rhymes;
now the truth is the biggest lie,
so we cross the Limpopo, and die.

VIA DOLOROSA

'How far is it from Olive Mount
to the place they call
Golgotha?' asks the teenage girl
with a tennis ball-

sized foetus in her womb, rugby
ball-sized baby wrapped
in swaddling offcuts on her back;
vitality sapped

by stinking fistula, tetters,
itching warts, herpes…
'It's also known as Calvary.'
Whenever she sees

a man she buckles like a card-
board box, and trembles.
They found her by the Trade Fair grounds
where the river spills

its horror on Bulawayo;
where broken bottles and plastic
bags, used condoms, faeces, mutate
into a spastic

objective correlative. 'Skulls,'
she keeps muttering,
'the place of skulls; how much further?'
She begins to sing:

'How far is it from Olive Mount
to the place they call…
place they call…' then she goes silent,
and resumes her fall.

They flopped them on a wheelbarrow,
and trundled the three
along Via Dolorosa,
to eternity.

VENDOR AND CHILD

Is that a shower of gold seeping
through gaps in the thatching of the sky?
What carefully wafting flakes are these
of light on fire, fading, to die

before they touch the woman and child
encamped beneath a municipal
cassia, now leafless, almost stripped
of life-transfusing bark? And when will

we halt beside her meagre tuckshop:
an upturned Lobels biscuit carton:
and buy a cigarette, a handful
of peanuts, and a blighted onion?

She cleared a space opposite the NO
STOPPING sign on Cecil Avenue,
a space she shares with sparrow weavers
bickering, and Matabele ants

that sting, and stink of formic acid,
with mandibles that nip the tendons
of her battered feet, and bear away,
piece by piece, the crumbs of her domain.

Sick, her child is the colour of ash,
a rag doll of hopelessness, symbol
of the new Zimbabwe. Who will buy
a soft tomato from me? Who will
deliver me from a government

of patronage, of cronyism;
a government of the obese, by
the obese, for the obese? Wallets

of flesh on the backs of their necks, folds
of fat behind their knees; like jumping
castles their bums, like teeming purses
their scrota. O who will deliver

us from these who have been coaxed into
temptation? And who will let that slow
light linger, those wafting flakes of fire,
and set the mother and her child aglow?

Bring Back Our Girls

Davids are Goliaths in waiting -

the corrupting effect of power.

It's a maxim worth re-stating,

re-considering, re-contemplating.

They kidnap then they deflower.

Davids are Goliaths in waiting.

Listen to their molars grating

as they disembowel, devour…

It's a maxim worth re-stating.

Forced fellating, forced mating,

let the bitches cower.

Davids are Goliaths in waiting.

Make them ululate, make them sing,

make their sweetness sicken to sour.

It's a maxim worth re-stating.

Bring back our girls! Bring them back! Bring!
Break the steeple, the rod, the tower.
David's are Goliaths in waiting:
It's a maxim worth re-stating.

CULTURE

'Culture is one of the two or three most complicated words in the English language.'   Raymond Williams

Culture is a patterned carpet, home to dust and mites

and unpleasant smells that linger.

Tom cat piss is the worst.

Culture gives you elbow rashes and itchy flea bites,

scratches from picked toe and finger-

nails. Carpets are cursed

with every stain and smear in the book of "Handy Hints."

Sometimes they enhance the patterns,

individualize,

like my old carpet, with its pets-and-children imprints;

threadbare, pocked with cooking-oil burns,

and rips like hornbill's cries.

When someone smugly says, "In our culture we do this!"

I recall a stink of carpets worse than Tom cat piss.

BROKE-BUTTOCK BLUES

They beat me with branches wrapped up in barb-wire,
they beat me with branches wrapped up in barb-wire;
my baby she crying, her face is on fire.

They say you are sell-out, you vote Tsvangirai,
they say you are sell-out, you vote Tsvangirai;
my baby, she dying, please God, tell me why?

They beat first my head then my back then my bums,
they beat first my head then my back then my bums;
they laugh and they say is like playing the drums.

I beg them for water, they say go ask Blair,
I beg them for water, they say go ask Blair.
Please, put out the fire in Mucheche's hair?

My bottom is broken, can not sit or stand,
my bottom is broken, can not sit or stand;
Mucheche can't breathe with her mouth in the sand.

They burned all our mealies, our chickens, our dog,
they burned all our mealies, our chickens, our dog;
my uncle, they hit him to death with a log.

For hours they beat me, for hours I cry,
for hours they beat me, for hours I cry;
please God, save my baby, do not let her die?

When they leave, like a tortoise I crawl very slow,
when they leave, like a tortoise I crawl very slow;
but my baby stopped crying a long time ago,
mwana wangu stopped crying a long time ago.

GHOSTLY GALLEON

A ghostly galleon plies the seas
that give and take, build and break
on Africa's ex-colonies:
on Mozambique, Namibia,
(sometimes mild and sometimes wild),
Angola and South Africa.

Bang, bang, bang, the An Yue Jiang
is looking for a port,
but workers on the Durban docks
said, "Nothing of the sort!

'Take your AKs somewhere else,
your mortars and grenades;
they'll use those bullets on working folk,
boys with dreadlocks and girls with braids,
waiters, vendors, gardeners, maids,
labourers with picks and spades,
farmers dragging the oxens' yoke.'

There is a ghostly galleon
that plies the southern seas;
it carries death for working folk:
cannons and RPGs.

It tried to dock in Durban
to drop its deadly load,
but the Durban Dockers' Union
upheld the workers' code.

Well it's a bang, bang, bang, the An Yue Jiang
Is sailing round the Cape
with toys for the Boys that make a loud noise,
that kill and maim and rape.

Salute the Durban Dockers
salute those workers bold:
they saved a thousand comrades
from misery untold.
They saved a thousand comrades,
but only for a day:
the ghostly galleon will be back –
terror is here to stay.

WAITING

I count the falling frangipani leaves.
Early April, the nights are growing cold;
the scent of wood smoke sours as neighbours burn
their household rubbish; every now and then
a discarded aerosol can explodes
triggering memories of another time,
another place, another war.

So quickly do they change from fluid green
to yellowish, to desiccated brown;
and yet, the drop, the clatter, ages takes;
takes ages: either way. In terminal
cymes some flowers remain, as white as wax,
mingling the bitter sweets of paradise
with odours of anxiety.

Like sharpening blades on steel the plovers cry
as homeless people wander near their nests
waiting for news, waiting for results. Who
will it be? These falling leaves remind me
that the day has come and gone for ballots
to be counted, results announced, and I'm
afraid that change will never come.

SICK AT HEART

Late one morning I walked the night;
not only was the sky alight
with Scorpio, and fireflies,
and owls with disembodied eyes;
but scattered widely in the dust
a million diamonds keen as lust.

A million spiders' eyes reflect
my headlamp, and then I detect
ten million termites loading grass:
a mass oblation comes to pass:
upheavals of the motherland:
close the pits with shovels of sand.

Orion killed by Scorpio,
his dying light, his afterglow;
that tilting of the Southern Cross,
Eros spilling Thanatos;
bushfires dimming an errant moon,
the sennet wind a loud bassoon.

Late one morning, walking the night
like Dickens after Esther's plight,
a stranger, undirected, hurled
against an unforgiving world,
yet mindful of our mother's womb,
which doubles as a common tomb;

mindful too of shovelling sand
in rhythms of a saraband,
grand, triple time, long second beat,
laying to rest just so much meat.
Hear it clattering on the planks
of coffins - for this relief, much thanks.

AN AWKWARD GAIT

Papa, Daddy, Uncle, Dear Old Man:
what is it about dictators that we
coddle them with terms of affection?
The lion will slaughter, and even eat,
cubs of his rivals. No subordinate
stands in the way of the dominant
white-browed sparrow weaver, the ballast
of whose gonads gives him an awkward flight.

Why do we admire Generals, pity
vendors? Why do we revere lions,
laugh at rock rabbits? What is it about
the clenched fist, the conical tower, church
steeples, pyramids, codpieces, that we
adore? Now this Autocrat, the ballast
of whose honorary doctorates gives
him: Uncle, Dear Old Man: an awkward gait.

AFRIKA

'Do you think, by spelling it with a "k",
that you will make it… well… more African?
that calling it Robert Mugabe Way
instead of Grey Street (what's in a man?)
the vendors squatting underneath the sign
will somehow earn more money down the line?'

'Look, friend, sacrifices have to be made …
I lost a favourite uncle in the war;
my post-doctoral thesis was delayed;
I'm still… well… relatively speaking, poor.
Rome – it's your round – wasn't built in a day…
Let's make a start… let's spell it with a "k".'

MALNOURISHED SONNET

The unburnt pot

on my desk

could never carry water

from the Umzingwane Dam,

or beer brewed

in a forty gallon drum,

or the spirit

of a stillborn baby;

but it is a useful receptacle

for my pen,

screwdriver,

tweezers,

nail clippers,

and Ingrid Jonker medal.

DOG

His father told him:
'If you can't piss in your own garden
you aren't a man.'
He pissed on Matabeleland.

As a senior pupil
at a private boarding school,
he nearly drowned a junior
with the contents of his bladder.

At Dubai World in Cape Town
(facilitating the acquisition of land in Zimbabwe
with his friend, the Minister),
he pissed in the wash basin.

He pissed on the wall,
he pissed on the toilet roll.
He said: 'There's mess in your bathroom.
Get your wog to clean it.'

CRUNCH TIME

Chongololos underfoot,
tiny anthills on the lawn,
stubbled fields,
carrots rinsed at the garden tap,
rusks without coffee -

waiting for results.

Pigs in the orchard,
hyenas at the skinning place,
liquidity,
skulls of protesters,
boots on the ground -

waiting for results.

THE CLOTHES DICTATORS WEAR

Cloth creases, even worsted, with old age;
tones, even tyrants', turn cataract blue;
the folded hanky, stained with rheum; the shame

of water marks upon the fly; the rage
of effeminate fists inclined to slew,
limp-wristed, around gatherings of lame

duck eggheads that feed Zimbabwe to gold
diggers, carpetbaggers, corporations
with logos that excite children, excite

mistresses with gross appetites for old
holders of fierce contending nations,
feral dogs dragging promise into night;

dragging suits more wrinkled, more vaguely hung,
no longer moving like a second skin
though once bespoke. But now the lily folds,

the prostate nudges the bladder, the lung
 is bunged, the lip minced; and the botox grin
like pressed cloth, dry-cleaning, coat hangers, holds,

holds an Italian design, choosy, slick:
a three-piece suit on a tottering stick.

MANIFESTO

In addition to our dear spouses
and our allocation of small houses,
we will have an escort in every town,
growth-point and village: novice, hand-me-down,
school girl, slut… whatever takes our fancy.
We will relegate to sties all nancy
boys, to kennels all dykes, who will be cured,
in God's good time, well and truly skewered,
by patriotic soldiers with long poles.
Sell-outs will be buried in ant bear holes
after overturning, or hitting trees.
All judges will be given factories
to asset-strip; and Generals will get mines,
with free access to anything that shines.
All policemen loyal to the Party
will be allowed to keep their bribes. Hearty
support will be given to servile priests,
and Chinese will be entertained with feasts
using cattle from sycophantic whites:
Rhodesians with insatiable appetites
for Four-by-fours, biltong, safari camps,
the nostalgic smell of paraffin lamps.
Aliens will be cast into outer
darkness. The First Lady will obtain her
beauty products from Harrods and Dubai.
We will encourage white people to die
because it's only then that we can trust
Blair's kith and kin. "Eternity or Bust"
Is our slogan. We affirm that bullets
are mightier than ballots, and true lies
make a nation healthy, wealthy, and wise.

We will double the strength of the forces,
give them live ammunition and horses
to crush traitors who disturb our cities
(especially girls who bare their titties.)
We will not tolerate freedom of speech,
freedom of assembly, freedom of each
and every citizen to criticize
our Excellency: all knowing; strong ties
with North Korea; Africa's Jesus!
Nations prostrate themselves when he sneezes,
and the world entire is shaken to bits
when Big Boy squats on his people – and shits.

THE DOG MEAT VENDOR

Salutations to the dog-meat vendor,
 he skins and guts the ones put down by vets;
his cuts, half rotten, are sweet and tender.

He sets no store by breed or gender,
 he traps no strays, he abducts no pets;
salutations to the dog-meat vendor.

Neither a borrower nor a lender,
 not too worried about whom he upsets;
his cuts, half rotten, are sweet and tender.

The one at the helm, the great pretender,
has plunged his people into untold debts;
salutations to the dog-meat vendor.

No one places blame on this offender;
starving citizens must have no regrets
His cuts, half rotten, are sweet and tender.

This villanelle has just one agenda:
appreciate what poverty begets.
His cuts, half rotten, are sweet and tender.
Salutations to the dog-meat vendor.

FOR THE DISAPPEARED

For those who burn or float face down, what tears;
what family protests smashed by rifle butts;
what withered whispers in what wasted ears,
of spilling, like beans, the brains and the guts?
For those in anthills or in mine shafts stuffed
like unironed washing, load on jumbled load
(one still in rusty leg-irons, one handcuffed),
what bells, what bugles, what intended ode?

But vigils, tongueless, levitate the night
while Law-and-Orders' boots respond to spit,
and somewhere in a rural hut, a light
is casting restless shadow-shapes that flit
and flicker, not fading before the dawn,
but waiting, like winking coals, to be born.

OBNUBILATION*

I say, what's happening to our nation
as clouds, like camouflage, obscure the sky,
is nothing short of obnubilation.
Six died, and more, much more than six will die.

I say, what's happening to Zimbabwe
as perspex shields reflecting someone's fear,
tapped by batons outside Hotel Bronte,
with gas and water cannon in the rear,

are by an indistinct transparency
a sign of what has been, what is, will be.

*the process or fact of making dimmer darker, or obscure

SOFT AS WOOL

But knit that wool into a scarf
in colours of your country's flag,
long, like the neck of a giraffe,
thick, like quality carpet shag;

more stubborn than a hangman's rope,
more cruel than piano wire,
more frightening than a lycanthrope.

DISCONNECTED POLICEMAN

His belt, tightened to the last notch,
danced like a fangless cobra;
his regulation boots had leering gaps
where toes, too sockless for words, bunched.
He had the complexion of a mummified
crocodile. I declined his offer of a pangolin scale.

MOTHER NATURE'S WARNING

I heard a plaintive cry on high,
it drained me to the marrow;
I looked, saw hornbills floating by,
raked me like a harrow.

Like swaying kites they tease the wind,
no strings to draw them down;
their message is that those who've sinned,
in countryside or town,

those dressed in camouflage, or blue,
or three-piece suits bespoke;
or curly wigs, who need not queue,
are going up in smoke.

These bushfire birds have come to town,
their message is quite clear:
he that wears the hollow crown
will waste in his despair.

MY UNCLE THE MINISTER

My uncle the Minister, is a such a meany,
 gave me a Jeep instead of a Lamborghini.
His name is Mafuta, his friends call him Fatti,
he visits his 'small houses' in a Bugatti.
His girl friends have Mercs, his children Rolls Royces –
they say he is dying of too many choices.
Indeed he looks poorly, that chalky complexion,
takes pills for his ulcers and for his erection.
Our family worries that if Uncle should die
we'd forfeit our slice of the Government pie,
a diminishing pie – parastatals are dead,
no tax base to speak of, pension schemes in the red.
 But, Uncle Mafuta, we trust, has a plan,
his slogan, you know, is 'Ehe, yes I can!'
And if I know my Uncle, he's still got the 'balls'
to invade and occupy Victoria Falls.

NO TIME TO BLEED

My cat's claws sound like dripping rain
as they prink, prink, my counterpane.
Dripping rain is what we need,
not blood. This is no time to bleed.

But listen to that eagle cry
what might have been a lullaby.
Socks and shoes is what we need,
not blood. This is no time to bleed.

And listen to that donkey bray
what might have been a roundelay.
Buttered bread is what we need,
Not blood. This is no time to bleed.

Oh listen to that cricket fret
what might have been a minuet.
Paraffin is what we need,
Not blood. This is no time to bleed.

THE BALLAD OF PROPHET SQUEEGEE

The Mormons got it wrong, you know,
the prophets still keep growing,
like fungal itch from toe to toe
or roadkill donkeys blowing.

This prophet called himself Squeegee,
his smile clinked ear with ear;
the doctrine of prosperity
transposed it to a leer.

The gift of healing in his hands,
his ankles and his thighs;
his hips, his nostrils, and his glands
begot orgasmic cries.

His best friend was the Holy Ghost,
they chatted on the phone,
quaffed wine together, chewed the Host,
loved making members moan.

He made girls lick his sweaty chin,
suck tears from his eyes;
they let him put his "devil" in
the "hell" between their thighs.

WHO IS PROTECTING THEM?
They call us maShurugwi,
our souls are made of mud;
our bodies live in mine-shafts,
our pangas drip the blood.

Voetseki maporisa,
hokoyo MDC,
masoja, tiza! tiza!*
mabhudhi we are free.

WIND BEHAVING BADLY

The clouds descend, the firmament grows grey,
a churning wind, bone-cold, assaults the trees,
blowing petals and little girls away
before relaxing to a shirtless breeze.
Again it rises flapping doeks and scarves,
banging casements, matrons, widows, wives...
whistling through cracks, keyholes, while it carves
that look in daddy's eyes. Run for your lives.
The clouds ascend, the firmament blows blue,
the rising wind lifts skirts and lashes hair—
what's true is false, my child, what's false is true—
the white sheets shaking, raking underwear.
Behaving-badly-winds will not subside
till you, my dears, commit tyrannicide.

ENGLISH SONNET IN BROKEN METRE

When capitalism fails the rich
(it always fails the poor), a jism
reinvigorates the corporate bitch:
let's call it bow-wow socialism.
Good ol' Uncle Sam, he saves the big banks
with tax-payers' money, tax-payers' sweat;
Wall Street billionaires, give him thanks
for winkling you fraudsters out of debt!
Dogknot socialism for plutocrats,
the broker-dealers' contingency plan;
ill-gotten gains made by ill-gotten brats
devilling themselves in the frying pan.
Where Bob's your uncle, the Reserve Bank feeds
cronyism, and the First Lady's needs.

THE HONOURABLE MINISTER SPEAKS

Yes, indeed, we have a culture of blame,
which we blame on colonialism;
we have sanctions, which we blame on the West;
we have floods and droughts, which we blame on rich
nations; we have sickness and poverty
and misery, which we blame on the white

  settlers who purloined our land (bled us white!)
by farming it, mining it... and we blame
them for writing poems on poverty
in Africa. Colonialism
has crippled our dear motherland, once rich
beyond riches: north to south, east to west,

you name it. But now, it has all gone west,
finished; our rites, traditions, have been white-
washed. 'We gave you football,' you say. That's rich!
'There's no accountability. You blame
corruption on colonialism.
Doesn't that indicate a poverty

of ideas?' No, my friend, Poverty,
inflicted on us by your men at West-
minster, reared by colonialism,
nurtured by imperialism, white
on black racism. "'Whatever you blame,'"
you quote, "'that you have done yourself.'" No rich

bitch murungu understands or cares. Rich
bitches like you, the queens of poverty,
consumers of black cock - you are to blame.
Like your Hollywood prototype, Mae West,
you want everything! Fuck off, back to White-
hall: patron of colonialism,

protector of colonialism,
donator of crumbs, which fall from the rich
man's table. You sicken me, sipping your white
wine, snacking, eyeing my crotch. Poverty
in Africa sustains the greedy West.
J'accuse. You, your kith and kin, are to blame.

Yes, colonialism is to blame,

monstrous child of your rich, decadent West.

The crime of poverty is coloured white.

Five Five-Line Stanzas

And they're all men
these prophets with their three-piece suits,
dark glasses,
Italian-styled shoes;

and they persuade you,
yes you! to drink their urine,
lick their sweat,
breathe insecticide.

 Why? Why do you do it?
You nouveau riche
who already have enough money,
 thanks to your connections,
to go on shopping sprees

to Dubai, Singapore, Johannesburg,
occasionally even to Harrods.
Orgasmic moaning when he speaks to God
 on his smart phone,
 when he puts his devil in your hell.

How easy then is it
for our politicians
to convince you
that they are in it
not for themselves but for you?

THOSE ABOUT TO PLAY

Celebrities are the gladiators
of neoliberalism.
they don't fight fires,
they don't fight floods,
they don't fight disease,
they fight each other.

They fight each other
in coliseums
like Hollywood,
the Super Bowl,
Madison Square Gardens,
Cable News Network.

The Masters of the universe
use them to distract
the poor in spirit,
the meek,
the merciful,
the peacemakers.

Ave, Imperator,
qui ad ludere,
te salutant.

BRATS

They wear dark glasses that make a statement;
their white denims are even more distressed
than the old folk at Edith Duly Home.
Those high-top sneakers, ideal for clubbing,
for trashing, for swigging, from the bottle,
Moet & Chandon Dom Perignon White Gold,
while their elders back home queue for putrid
dog meat, road-kill, discarded cabbage leaves.

On social media they brag, faces
already beginning to twist and bloat,
bragging to their thousands of admirers
that they are immune from prosecution,
like their progenitors, above the law.
These our sons! They post a flame emoji,
the evening is lit, the government
aides are hovering. You and I will pay.

YET ANOTHER FLOWER POEM

The American Dream is uncovered for being just that

in the flowers of the poinsettia, which are not flowers

at all but a series of scarlet bracts or modified leaves.

They recall the lips of Hollywood stars like Rita Hayworth,

and, most poignantly, of America's astounding poet,

Sylvia Plath. But this is my garden in Bulawayo!

What has the American Dream or "manifest destiny"

got to do with it? Everything, I guess; except our clichés

are different, like "Commonwealth of Nations", "rod of empire",

"Rule Britannia". And this shrub, Euphorbia pulcherrima,

adorning my early winter garden, concordant with that

afterglow of common thatching grass unsettling as its "flowers",

is as much a settler as I am; and the day that it leaves

is the day I leave: "For I have neither wit, nor words, nor worth",

as politicians have, and academics (a white poet

should restrict his content to the flora of Bulawayo),

"to stir men's (sic) blood". My settler friends and me, our destiny is obscure. We measure out our lives in platitudes, clichés,

watching the sun set on Zimbabwe, as it set on empire:

scarlet and gold, heart-breaking, most beautiful -
pulcherrima.

THE COMING OF THE RAINS

Romantics like Rousseau talk nonsense
when they insist that we are born free,
though he's right about the chains. See,
you didn't know which side of the fence

you would end up attempting to climb.
You had no say in your spawning,
or the biology of your thing,
or your complexion. Yet time and time

again we are told of a free press,
a free state, free will, freedom of speech,
freedom to write what we like, to preach
what we like, freedom to make a mess.

"It's often safer to be in chains,"
says Franz Kafka, "than to be free."
But safety is not the issue, see –
it's the rains, the coming of the rains.

Epilogue

SEEKING IDENTITY

I look for my self
in family, friends,
home and garden,
grass, flowers, rocks, trees…

all the while resisting
my gender,
my skin colour,
my nationality.

Mmap New African Poets Series

If you have enjoyed *Pressed Flowers: Poems of Resistance* consider these other fine books in **New African Poets Series** from *Mwanaka Media and Publishing*:

I Threw a Star in a Wine Glass by Fethi Sassi
Best New African Poets 2017 Anthology by Tendai R Mwanaka and Daniel Da Purificacao
Logbook Written by a Drifter by Tendai Rinos Mwanaka
Mad Bob Republic: Bloodlines, Bile and a Crying Child by Tendai Rinos Mwanaka
Zimbolicious Poetry Vol 1 by Tendai R Mwanaka and Edward Dzonze
Zimbolicious: An Anthology of Zimbabwean Literature and Arts, Vol 3 by Tendai Mwanaka
Under The Steel Yoke by Jabulani Mzinyathi
Fly in a Beehive by Thato Tshukudu
Bounding for Light by Richard Mbuthia
Sentiments by Jackson Matimba
Best New African Poets 2018 Anthology by Tendai R Mwanaka and Nsah Mala
Words That Matter by Gerry Sikazwe
The Ungendered by Delia Watterson
Ghetto Symphony by Mandla Mavolwane
Sky for a Foreign Bird by Fethi Sassi
A Portrait of Defiance by Tendai Rinos Mwanaka
When Escape Becomes the only Lover by Tendai R Mwanaka
ويَسهَرُ اللَّيلُ عَلى شَفَتي...وَالغَمَام by Fethi Sassi
A Letter to the President by Mbizo Chirasha
Righteous Indignation by Jabulani Mzinyathi:
Blooming Cactus By Mikateko Mbambo
Rhythm of Life by Olivia Ngozi Osouha

Travellers Gather Dust and Lust by Gabriel Awuah Mainoo
Chitungwiza Mushamukuru: An Anthology from Zimbabwe's Biggest Ghetto Town by Tendai Rinos Mwanaka
Because Sadness is Beautiful? by Tanaka Chidora

Soon to be released

Of Bloom Smoke by Abigail George
Denga reshiri yokunze kwenyika by Fethi Sassi
Shades of Black by Edward Dzonze

https://facebook.com/MwanakaMediaAndPublishing/

www.ingramcontent.com/pod-product-compliance
Lightning Source LLC
Chambersburg PA
CBHW011952150426
43196CB00019B/2919